W0246784

the little book of
IKIGAI

Copyright © 2025 Headline Publishing Group Limited

The right of Victoria Denne to be identified as the Author of the Work has been asserted by her in accordance with the Copyright, Designs and Patents Act 1988.

First published in 2025 by OH
An Imprint of HEADLINE PUBLISHING GROUP LIMITED

2

Disclaimer:
All trademarks, copyright, quotations, company names, registered names, products, characters, logos and catchphrases used or cited in this book are the property of their respective owners.

Apart from any use permitted under UK copyright law, this publication may only be reproduced, stored, or transmitted, in any form, or by any means, with prior permission in writing of the publishers or, in the case of reprographic production, in accordance with the terms of licences issued by the Copyright Licensing Agency.

Cataloguing in Publication Data is available from the British Library

ISBN 978-1-03542-273-9

Compiled and written by: Victoria Denne
Editorial: Saneaah Muhammad
Designed and typeset in Avenir by: Stephen Cary
Project manager: Russell Porter
Production: Arlene Lestrade
Printed and bound in Dubai

Headline's policy is to use papers that are natural, renewable and recyclable products and made from wood grown in well-managed forests and other controlled sources. The logging and manufacturing processes are expected to conform to the environmental regulations of the country of origin.

HEADLINE PUBLISHING GROUP LIMITED
An Hachette UK Company
Carmelite House, 50 Victoria Embankment, London EC4Y 0DZ

The authorised representative in the EEA is Hachette Ireland, 8 Castlecourt Centre, Dublin 15, D15 XTP3, Ireland (email: info@hbgi.ie)

www.headline.co.uk   www.hachette.co.uk

the little book of
IKIGAI

victoria denne

CONTENTS

INTRODUCTION

In a world that feels ever more hurried and disjointed, the concept of **ikigai** shines out like a beacon of hope.

Rooted in Japanese culture and imbued with nuances the English language is unable to fully convey, the true meaning of *ikigai* is hard to pin down.

Whether we translate it as the purpose, meaning, value of life or even "the reason we get out of bed in the morning", at its core, it is the belief that a life lived with purpose and meaning leads to greater fulfilment, happiness and wellbeing.

This little book serves as a window into this enigmatic philosophy, first introducing the concept of *ikigai*, its various definitions and modern interpretations, before exploring its Japanese origins.

After delving into *ikigai*'s benefits, both physical and mental, it also provides practical tips to help integrate the concept into your own life.

Throughout, we will hear words of wisdom and advice from the preeminent *ikigai* experts, as well as figures who unknowingly practise *ikigai*

and espouse some of its central tenants such as slowing down, savouring the small moments of joy in life and remembering that life is about the journey, not the destination.

Whether you're looking for a new direction in life or seeking more fulfilment in the everyday, this book will shed light on a timeless practice that will help you uncover what truly makes your life worth living.

CHAPTER

1

WHAT IS
IKIGAI?

生き甲斐

ikigai

iki, meaning "to exist", and **kai**, meaning "worth" or "value".

"The first thing you have to learn is how to pronounce it. It's pronounced **ee-key-guy**.

You lift your cheeks like you're smiling… It's not pronounced icky-guy."

Tim Tamashiro
TED Talk: "How to Ikigai", June 2018

While there is no direct English equivalent, *ikigai* is often translated as

a reason for being

or

life's purpose

– perhaps because it is a more familiar concept in the West.

Many other translations have been offered, which all try to capture its multifaceted meaning.

They include:

the fruits of life

the reward for existing

the value of life

a reason to live

a life worth living

Ikigai is similar to the French term *raison d'etre* or "reason for being".
It is also linked to the Greek idea of *eudaimonia*, a life well-lived.

There is some consensus that its concept of purpose has both personal and social dimensions – this is illustrated in the well-known Ikigai Venn Diagram, created by Marc Winn.

that which you
love

passion

mission

that
which
you are
good
at

ikigai

that
which
the
world
needs

profession

vocation

that which you
can be paid for

As you can see, the diagram includes overlapping spheres that encompass:

what you love to do

what you are good at

what the world needs

what you can get paid for

Within this diagram, *ikigai* sits at the sweet spot right at the centre: it is a combination of something that you love, that you are good at, that the world needs and that people will pay you for.

From this diagram we could also
extrapolate the following:

Your
passion
lies at the
intersection of
what you love
and
**what you are
good at.**

Your

mission

lies at the
intersection of
what you love
and
**what the
world needs.**

Your
vocation
lies at the
intersection of
**what the
world needs**
and
**what you can get
paid for.**

Your
profession
lies at the
intersection of
**what you are
good at.**
and
**what you can get
paid for.**

The diagram was popularized by
Albert Liebermann and Hector Garcia,
who presented it as a way of applying
ikigai in their book, *Ikigai: The Japanese
Secret to a Long and Happy Life*.

However, while the Ikigai Venn Diagram might be helpful in deciding what to devote one's life to in terms of profession, there is a general consensus that it represents a Westernized understanding of the Japanese concept, and that its focus on one's career does **not** convey the true meaning of *ikigai*.

In fact, Marc Winn, who is credited as the creator of this now somewhat famous diagram, has gone on to explain more about its origins since its surge in popularity:

"In 2014, I wrote a blog post on the subject of Ikigai. In that blog post, I merged two concepts to create something new. Essentially, I merged a Venn diagram on 'purpose' with Dan Buettner's Ikigai concept, in relation to living to be more than 100.

The sum total of my effort was that I changed one word on a diagram and shared a 'new' meme with the world."

Marc Winn

So, leaving the Venn diagram aside,
how do we go about defining what
ikigai truly is, and, in turn, find out
what our own version of it might
look like?

To do this, we must return to its roots
and understand what *ikigai* means
to the people of Japan.

CHAPTER

2

the ORIGINS
of
IKIGAI

According to clinical psychologist and Associate Professor **Akihiro Hasegawa**, the origins of the word *ikigai* trace back to the Heian period (794–1185), which was considered a high point in Japanese culture.

According to Hasegawa:

"**Gai** *comes from the word* **kai** *('shell' in Japanese)," he says, "which were deemed highly valuable, and from there* **ikigai** *derived as a word that means* **value in living**."

As Hasegawa points out, the word **life** in English can mean both **lifetime** and **everyday life**, which is worth bearing in mind when we translate **ikigai** as **life's purpose**.

In Japan, there is **jinsei**, which means lifetime, and **seikatsu**, which means **everyday life**.

Hasegawa suggests that **ikigai** aligns more with the latter.

So, while *ikigai* can have elements of one's larger **purpose in life**, it may be more accurate to understand *ikigai* as **the value to be found in everyday life**.

For most Japanese people, therefore, *ikigai* is about discovering the small, everyday joys that, when added together, make life more **fulfilling** as a whole.

"The majority of the Japanese people regard ikigai to be something simple, like joy in everyday life."

Sachiaki Takamiya

"Ikigai *is about focusing on individual moments, not just on the big journey of life.*"

Yukari Mitsuhashi

Some have translated *ikigai* as "the reason you get up in the morning".

When we consider both the larger and smaller everyday living elements contained within *ikigai*, this "reason" might take the form of a job to do, a child to care for, a person to love or a cup of tea to sip and enjoy.

"It could be something very small like having a cup of coffee and chocolate, and it is something that makes your day go on. That is ikigai. On the other hand – ikigai can be a life-defining, very big goal, like going to Mars or winning the Nobel Prize or becoming the Prime Minister of a country. So ikigai can be something small or something big."

Ken Mogi

Since *ikigai* can be found throughout life, from the smallest moments to the largest, Ken Mogi describes it as a spectrum:

"The complexity of ikigai actually reflects the complexity of life itself. So, in order to be a master of ikigai, you really need to appreciate how complex and rich life actually is."

Ken Mogi

In Japan, *ikigai* is not taught.

Instead, it is an inherent way of life, passed down from generation to generation.

"The Japanese do not need grandiose motivational frameworks to keep going, but rely more on the little rituals in their daily routines."

Ken Mogi
*Awakening Your Ikigai:
How the Japanese Wake Up to Joy and
Purpose Every Day*

CHAPTER

3

FINDING
YOUR
IKIGAI

While *ikigai* has been a feature of Japanese culture for centuries, it was popularized by **Mieko Kamiya**, a doctor, psychiatrist and author known as the "Mother of Ikigai Psychology".

One of the first researchers of *ikigai*, Kamiya interviewed patients suffering from leprosy at a sanatorium on Nagashima Island and tried to identify why some patients seemed more happy and content, despite their condition, while others did not.

Kamiya's book,

On the Meaning of Life,

has never been translated into English, although perhaps this will not be the case for much longer, given the recent renewed interest in *ikigai*.

Through her research, Kamiya believed that there were two elements to the lived experience of *ikigai*:

the

object

of *ikigai*

and...

the
feeling
inspired by
their object of
ikigai.

"There are two ways of using the word ikigai. *When someone says 'this child is my* ikigai,' *it refers to the source or target of the* ikigai… *and when one feels* ikigai *as a state of mind –* ikigai-kan."*

Mieko Kamiya

Kamiya's
7 needs

Kamiya went on to identify seven conditions, or needs, that must be satisfied in order to experience *ikigai-kan* – the **feeling** of ikigai.

1. the need for **life satisfaction**
2. the need for **change and growth**
3. the need for **a bright future**
4. the need for **resonance**
5. the need for **freedom**
6. the need for **self-actualization**
7. the need for **meaning and value**

Professor Akihiro Hasegawa suggests combining the two elements of *ikigai*, the **object** and the **feeling**, to experience its true form:

"the feeling that we are alive in the here and now, and the individual awareness that drives us to survive."

With this in mind, Hasegawa suggests those searching for *ikigai* cultivate deep connections with their loved ones and dedicate time to finding activities that bring them meaning, purpose and joy in their everyday existence.

This chimes with what Professor Gordon Matthews says:

that

ikigai

is what
makes people's
lives worth living,
as well as the feeling of
being alive.

"I don't believe people are looking for the meaning of life as much as they are looking for the experience of being alive."

Joseph Campbell

WHERE

can you FIND

your IKIGAI?

As we've discussed, while the object of *ikigai* can be found in one's career, this is a rather limited, and limiting, understanding of the concept.

In a survey of Japanese men and women conducted in 2010:

75%

of the 2,000 respondents claimed that they had *ikigai*, but only **a third** said that this was related to their **work**.

Apart from one's job, there are multiple spheres in which to find *ikigai*, including:

- **hobbies**
- **social interactions**
- **close relationships**
- **voluntary activities**

"Ikigai *is what makes
life worth living, and it's
something in your social
world. It can be your
family, your work, a hobby
you're passionately devoted
to, or a religious belief.*"

Gordon Matthews

It doesn't have to be found in one area alone, either; it can come from multiple sources. And, importantly, it can change over time.

What constitutes or gives us the feeling of *ikigai* today might not be the same ten years from now – in fact, it probably won't be.

As we go through life's ups and downs, what gives meaning to our lives will change. Just as we grow and evolve, *ikigai* does the same

"Just like all things are transient, all ikigai is precarious. It does vanish, it will always vanish at the end of the day. Nonetheless, having it is worth it."

Gordon Matthews

"Ikigai *is something that makes me feel human, and makes me feel glad to be alive.*"

Makoto Rexrode

One of the myths of *ikigai* is that it must encompass something "that the **world needs**".

This is not so.

*"You may feel a lot
of value in your life by
contributing to society.
It is possible that what the
world needs from you is
your ikigai, but it doesn't
have to be."*

Sachiaki Takamiya

To find one's **object**
of *ikigai*, Sachiaki Takamiya
recommends asking yourself
important questions,
such as:

"What do I want to achieve?"

and:

*"How
do I want to
spend
my time?"*

From there, he says, you will gain a
better understanding of your

true self

and uncover your

life's purpose.

Another myth is that *ikigai* must be found in something you

"**love to do**".

You may not love your work, for example, but that doesn't mean you can't find meaning in it.

"Ikigai *can be about finding meaning in something. It doesn't have to be something that you love.*"

Nicholas Kemp

"Ikigai *resides in the realm of small things. The morning air, the cup of coffee, the ray of sunshine, the massaging of octopus meat and the American president's praise are on equal footing. Only those who can recognize the richness of this whole spectrum really appreciate and enjoy it.*"

Ken Mogi
*Awakening Your Ikigai:
How the Japanese Wake Up to Joy and
Purpose Every Day*

When it comes to finding your own *ikigai*, Ken Mogi suggests a good place to start is to ask yourself the following two questions:

"What are your most sentimental values?"

and:

*"What are
the small things
that give
you pleasure?"*

"Although a grand mission is admirable and, with perseverance, might be achievable, starting small and seeing the impact you're making will enable you to find meaning in what you do and give you a stronger sense of purpose So you might feel a desire to solve world hunger, but you could help in a more specific way by volunteering at a local food bank. This gives your something tangible to focus on."

Yukari Mitsuhashi

"Ikigai *is what, day after day and year after year, each of us most essentially lives for.*"

Gordon Mathews

CHAPTER
4

the FIVE PILLARS of IKIGAI

"If you can make the process of making the effort your primary source of happiness, then you have succeeded in the most important challenge of your life."

Ken Mogi

Tokyo-based neuroscientist and author
Ken Mogi identifies

5 central pillars

of ikigai.

central pillar one

STARTING
SMALL

This is associated with the concept of **kodawari**, where craftspeople take incredible care in the finer details of their creations.

For the purposes of *ikigai*, it means take **small steps**, and don't worry about the end goal:

the **process** is the important part.

central pillar two

RELEASING YOURSELF

At its core, this is about **self-acceptance**.

When we learn to **accept** our true selves and the way we **wish** to live our lives,

contentment
is not far away.

central pillar three

HARMONY

and

SUSTAIN-ABILITY

This pillar encompasses our **relationship** with others as well as the world we live in.

Our actions have **consequences**, and we must be

mindful

of them always.

central pillar four

the JOY of
LITTLE
THINGS

To make sure you are noticing the good things all around you, embed **joyful experiences** into your everyday routine.

That way, no matter what else goes wrong that day, you still have these mini moments of

happiness

to enjoy.

central pillar five

BEING in the HERE and NOW

Take inspiration from **children** and concentrate **only** on the

present moment.

*"Ideally, every
social activity should be
sustainable."*

Ken Mogi

"When you take notice of the small details of life, nothing is repeated. Every opportunity is special."

Ken Mogi

CHAPTER
5

the BENEFITS of IKIGAI

the SECRET to HAPPINESS

"The grand essentials to happiness in this life are something to do, something to love, and something to hope for."

Héctor García
and
Francesc Miralles
Ikigai: The Japanese Secret to a Long and Happy Life

97

According to Professor Gordon Matthews, those who possess *ikigai* experience

greater happiness

compared to those without it, because it provides a profound

sense of purpose.

*"What I can say
in terms of psychological
judgement is if you have
ikigai, you probably are
considerably happier than
if you don't, because
it's something that you
live for."*

Gordon Matthews

"I think it's a key to happiness because I think people with ikigai are happy."

Makoto Rexrode

Japan is home to some of the **longest-living** citizens of the world, and many believe this in-built concept of *ikigai* may be a contributing factor.

the KEY to LONGEVITY

In their book, *Ikigai: The Japanese Secret to a Long and Happy Life*, Albert Liebermann and Hector Garcia propose

10 "rules" of living a good life,

which were gathered and distilled from conversations with some of the longest-living residents of Ogimi, a small village in Okinawa, Japan.

These rules are:

1. **Stay active; don't retire.**
2. **Take it slow.**
3. **Don't fill your stomach.**
4. **Surround yourself with good friends.**
5. **Get in shape.**
6. **Smile.**
7. **Reconnect with nature.**
8. **Give thanks.**
9. **Live in the moment.**
10. **Follow your *ikigai*.**

"According to scientists who have studied the five Blue Zones, the keys to longevity are diet, exercise, finding a purpose in life (an ikigai) and forming strong social ties – that is, having a broad circle of friends and good family relations."

Héctor García
and
Francesc Miralles
Ikigai: The Japanese Secret to a Long and Happy Life

Dan Buettner, who studies supposed **Blue Zones** – places in the world with an unusually high percentage of centenarians – has also highlighted the role *ikigai* plays in the longevity of those living on the island of Okinawa.

He also notes that, while it goes by a different name, this idea of a purpose or meaning to life is common to many other Blue Zones, including Sardinia and Nicoya Peninsula.

"*...in every Blue Zone, centenarians possess a strong sense of purpose. In Okinawa it was* ikigai *– the reason to wake up in the morning... the Costa Ricans called it* plan de vida."

Dan Buettner
The Blue Zones: 9 Lessons for Living Longer from the People Who've Lived the Longest

Due to this recent surge of interest in the Blue Zones, *ikigai* is often thought to go hand in hand with longevity, but this isn't really the case – at least, not intentionally.

We might instead say longevity is merely a happy byproduct of a life lived with meaning.

While it doesn't inherently contain any connotations of longevity, the concept of *ikigai* does originate in traditional Japanese medicine, a central tenant of which is that one's emotional and mental wellbeing has an effect on one's physical health.

a PHYSICAL HEALTH BOOST?

While numerous studies have shown that those who say they have an object or feeling of *ikigai* report higher life satisfaction and levels of happiness, there is even some evidence to suggest that these people have increased immune function, less anxiety and improved resilience.

In 2021, researchers in Japan took data from a nationwide longitudinal study of over 65s and found:

"Having ikigai (vs. not having ikigai) was associated with a 31% lower risk of developing functional disability and 36% lower risk of developing dementia during the three-year follow-up. Having ikigai was associated with decreased depressive symptoms and hopelessness as well as higher happiness, life satisfaction, instrumental activity of daily living, and certain social outcomes (e.g., more frequent participation in hobby clubs)."

Although more research
is needed to ascertain
causation, rather than
correlation, the evidence for
ikigai's health benefits seem
to be promising.

If, as many medical practitioners in the West are beginning to, we accept that our mental state affects our physical state, it doesn't seem such a leap to suggest that a philosophy that encourages people to seek joy and fulfilment in their everyday lives would lead to greater emotional wellbeing, and so, by extension, better physical health.

"Based on a number of meta-analyses and longitudinal studies, evidence suggests a protective benefit and positive correlation between ikigai *and better physical health, and an inverse relationship with all-cause mortality. Psychologically,* ikigai *may be important in developing one's sense of self-understanding, goal attainability, and problem-solving skills."*

Yasuhiro Kotera et al
Health Benefits of Ikigai: A Review of Literature (2021)

a SUPER-POWER?

In terms of its more general benefits, Yukari Mitsuhashi believes having a sense of *ikigai*:

"brings you focus and direction, and serves as an anchor in your life."

"With ikigai in mind, you will not have to think twice about what matters to you, and hence you will know what to prioritize. We are bombarded with endless decisions to be made day after day, but knowing your ikigai will eliminate your insecurities about your decisions and allow you to make better ones. Your will find that simple decisions, like how you spend your time, will automatically be made for you when you know your ikigai."

Yukari Mitsuhashi
Ikigai: Giving every day meaning and joy

"When you put your finger on what your ikigai is, it's like you gain a superpower. It's like you get a GPS for your life."

Tim Tamashiro

In our search for *ikigai*, we can also find out more about our true selves, what, or who, brings us

joy

and gives meaning to our days, and even what gives

purpose

to our lives as a whole.

"This word [ikigai] is really like a treasure map. And, this treasure map can help you find your way to finding wonderful things about yourself that you can share with the world, and the world will say 'thank you' for it."

Tim Tamashiro

CHAPTER

6

TOP TIPS for LIVING a LIFE of IKIGAI

STAY in the PRESENT MOMENT

"Ikigai *cannot be found in the future. It can only be lived in the now.*"

Tim Tamashiro

*"Be where you are;
otherwise you will miss
your life."*

Buddha

"We're so busy watching out for what's just ahead of us that we don't take time to enjoy where we are."

Bill Watterson

"Be happy in the moment,
that's enough.
Each moment is all we
need, not more."

Mother Teresa

"Most humans are never fully present in the now. Because unconsciously they believe that the next moment must be more important than this one. But then you miss your whole life, which is never not now."

Eckhart Tolle

"Living in the moment, that's the first step to Having."

Suh Yoon Lee

"Happiness, not in another place but this place... not for another hour, but this hour."

Walt Whitman

cultivate

GOOD RELATION- SHIPS

"Young people often say, 'My life has no ikigai.' This is obvious. People who isolate themselves can't have ikigai – meaning or purpose. Ikigai is only found in interpersonal relationships."

Ishikawa Tatsuzō

"Try to connect deeply with the people you care about in your relationships."

Prof. Akihiro Hasegawa

"Always remember that you are absolutely unique. Just like everyone else."

Margaret Mead

rediscover

NATURE
and SILENCE

"Because of technology, people have become very busy now. We're spending a lot of time online, and not spending enough time living in nature. This destroys out sense of how to feel things. This will make it hard for us to find our ikigai."

Eckhart Tolle

"In every walk with nature one receives far more than he seeks."

John Muir

"*Purpose requires self-knowledge which requires silence.*"

Maxime Lagacé

*"Look deep into nature,
and then you will
understand everything
better."*

Albert Einstein

"Leave the roads; take the trails."

Pythagoras

find MEANING in the SMALL as well as the BIG

*"If you cannot
do great things, do
small things
in a great way."*

Napoleon Hill

"The simple things are also the most extraordinary things, and only the wise can see them."

Paulo Coelho

"The greatest task for any person is to find meaning in his or her own life."

Victor Frankl

"The mystery of human existence lies not in just staying alive, but in finding something to live for."

Fyodor Dostoyevsky

"Man is a being in search of meaning."

Plato

FOLLOW your OWN PATH

no one else's

"Find out who you are and be that person. That's what your soul was put on this earth to be. Find the truth, live that truth, and everything else will come."

Ellen DeGeneres

"You define your own life. Don't let other people write your script."

Oprah Winfrey

"Find out who you are and do it on purpose."

Dolly Parton

"There is not one big cosmic meaning for all; there is only the meaning we each give to our life, an individual meaning, an individual plot, like an individual novel, a book for each person."

Anais Nin

"Forging a new path is far more satisfying than following a map will ever be."

James Pierce

LET GO of
PERFECTION

"*Life does not have to be perfect to be wonderful.*"

Annette Funicello

"'The greatest illusion,' said the mole, 'is that life should be perfect.'"

Charlie Mackesy
The Boy, the Mole, the Fox and the Horse

*"We must let go of the life
we have planned, so as
to accept the one that is
waiting for us."*

Joseph Campbell

"The purpose of life is not to be happy. It is to be useful, to be honorable, to be compassionate, to have it make some difference that you have lived and lived well."

Ralph Waldo Emerson

*"There is no perfection,
only life."*

Milan Kundera

HELP
OTHERS
if you CAN

*"We make a living
by what we get, but
we make a life
by what we give."*

Winston Churchill

*"One of the deep secrets
of life is that all that is
really worth the doing is
what we do for others."*

Lewis Carroll

*"One of the things we
need as a human beings is
a feeling of being needed."*

Makoto Rexrode

SAVOUR the MINOR MIRACLES

*"The way to develop the habit
of savoring is to pause when
something is beautiful and good
and catches our attention –
the sound of rain, the look
of the night sky – the glow
in a child's eyes, or when we
witness some kindness. Pause…
then totally immerse in the
experience of savouring it."*

Tara Brach

"I've always believed in savouring the moments. In the end, they are the only things we'll have."

Anna Godbersen

"All that is important is this one moment in movement. Make the moment important, vital and worth living. Do not let it slip away unnoticed and unused."

Martha Graham

"Take the time to enjoy the little things, for one day you may look back and realize they were the big things."

Robert Brault

*"Life isn't a matter
of milestones, but of
moments."*

Rose Kennedy

be GRATEFUL for WHAT you HAVE

"Happiness never comes to those who fail to appreciate what they already have."

Buddha

*"The more you practice
the art of thankfulness,
the more you have to be
thankful for."*

Norman Vincent Peale

"Gratitude is the ability to experience life as a gift. It liberates us from the prison of self-preoccupation."

John Ortberg

FOCUS on the PROCESS not the RESULT

"Life is a journey, not a destination."

Ralph Waldo Emerson

"So, what if, instead of thinking about solving your whole life, you just think about adding additional good things. One at a time. Just let your pile of good things grow."

Rainbow Rowell

"The purpose of life is to live it, to taste experience to the utmost, to reach out eagerly and without fear for newer and richer experience."

Eleanor Roosevelt

DISCOVER
your
PASSIONS

*"If you can't
figure out your
purpose, figure out
your passion.
For your passion
will lead you right into
your purpose."*

Bishop T. D. Jakes

"Pay attention to the things you are naturally drawn to. They are often connected to your path, passion and purpose in life. Have the courage to follow them."

Ruben Chavez

"Every life has a purpose. We need to let go of the past. Live in the present. Do not waste today worrying about what will happen tomorrow. Embrace your true spirit, embrace and listen to grace and be transformed in the moment. Do not fixate on what you want but give thanks for what you have."

Caroline Myss

*"Always go with
your passions. Never
ask yourself if
it's realistic or not."*

Deepak Chopra

*"The man who is born
with a talent, which he
is meant to use, finds
his greatest happiness in
using it."*

Johann Wolfgang von Goethe

LIVE with PURPOSE

"Purpose gives meaning to our being and purpose has myriad meanings for us."

Somali K. Chakrabarti

"The greatest tragedy is not death but life without purpose."

Rick Warren

"Your purpose is here
and now. Your purpose is
along the journey."

Sadie Robertson

"You are growth-seeking beings, and as you are moving forward, you are at your happiest."

Abraham Hicks

*"Life without a purpose
is like a body
without a soul."*

Unknown

CONCLUSION

The quest for
a life of greater
happiness and
fulfilment is
one shared by
all humans,
and
meaning
is often at
the heart of
this.

Meaning doesn't have to be world-altering for it to be important.

It doesn't matter whether you find your *ikigai* in big things, like discovering your vocation, or the small things, such as enjoying a coffee with your best friend.

What matters is that you **become aware** of these joys and **savour them** regularly.

*"Be happy for this moment.
This moment is your life."*

Omar Khayyam